Wearable Electronics

CHERRY LAKE PUBLISHING • ANN ARBOR, MICHIGAN

by Martin Gitlin

A Note to Adults: Please review the instructions for the activities in this book before allowing children to do them. Be sure to help them with any activities you do not think they can safely complete on their own.

A Note to Kids: Be sure to ask an adult for help with these activities when you need it. Always put your safety first!

Published in the United States of America by Cherry Lake Publishing
Ann Arbor, Michigan
www.cherrylakepublishing.com

Content Adviser: Matthew Lammi, PhD, Assistant Professor, College of Education, North Carolina State University, Raleigh, North Carolina
Reading Adviser: Marla Conn MS, Ed., Literacy Specialist, Read-Ability, Inc.
Photo Credits: Cover and page 1, ©Syda Productions/Shutterstock, Inc.; page 4, ©Tyler Olson/Shutterstock, Inc.; page 5, ©Monkey Business Images/Shutterstock, Inc.; page 7 ©anaken2012/Shutterstock, Inc.; page 8, ©Anna Hoychuk/Shutterstock, Inc.; page 10, ©Dragon Images/Shutterstock, Inc.; page 13, ©ASSOCIATED PRESS; page 14, ©Patti McConville/Alamy Stock Photo; page 15, ©Chris Strickland/Alamy Stock Photo; page 16, ©Melpomene/Shutterstock, Inc.; page 17, ©Richard Levine/Alamy Stock Photo; page 18, ©SpeedKingz/Shutterstock, Inc.; page 19, ©wavebreakmedia/Shutterstock, Inc.; page 21, ©Pressmaster/Shutterstock, Inc.; page 22, ©A. Aleksandravicius/Shutterstock, Inc.; page 23, ©dennizn/Shutterstock, Inc.; page 24, ©dpa picture alliance/Alamy Stock Photo; page 27, ©amstockphoto/Shutterstock, Inc.

Library of Congress Cataloging-in-Publication Data
Names: Gitlin, Marty, author.
Title: Wearable electronics / by Martin Gitlin.
Description: Ann Arbor, Michigan : Cherry Lake Publishing, [2018] | Series:
   Emerging technology | Series: 21st century skills innovation library |
   Includes bibliographical references and index. | Audience: Grades 4 to 6.
Identifiers: LCCN 2017000104| ISBN 9781634727051 [lib. bdg.] | ISBN
   9781634727716 [pdf] | ISBN 9781634727389 [pbk.] | ISBN 9781634728041
   [ebook]
Subjects: LCSH: Wearable technology—Juvenile literature.
Classification: LCC TK7820 .G58 2018 | DDC 621.381—dc23 LC record available at https://lccn.loc.gov/2017000104

Cherry Lake Publishing would like to acknowledge the work of the Partnership for 21st Century Learning. Please visit *www.p21.org* for more information.

Printed in the United States of America
Corporate Graphics

Contents

Chapter 1	**Past and Present**	4
Chapter 2	**The Fun Stuff**	10
Chapter 3	**Live and Learn**	16
Chapter 4	**For Your Health**	21
Chapter 5	**A Look into the Future**	26
	Glossary	30
	Find Out More	31
	Index	32
	About the Author	32

Chapter 1

Past and Present

We live in an exciting time for technology. It seems like cool new gadgets are coming out almost constantly. Many of the most interesting products to hit the market in recent years are electronic devices you can wear.

Wearable electronics serve many purposes. They are video games and toys. They are virtual playgrounds. They are learning devices. They are health

Many people use wearable devices to pay for things instead of using cash or credit cards.

Today's hearing aids are much smaller and work much better than earlier versions.

monitors. They are personal **odometers**. They are cameras. But they are not new. They have been around for more than a century.

Travel back in time to 1898. That was the year electrical **engineer** Miller Reese Hutchison invented the first wearable electronic. It was a hearing aid known as the Akouphone. It used electricity to make sounds louder. But it only worked if it was attached to a large tabletop machine. So much for leaving the house to visit friends!

The Amazing Ring of the 17th Century

Can you believe that a wearable calculator was invented nearly 500 years ago? The abacus was a counting tool used in China. A full-size abacus featured nine beads on each of 10 wires strung between two boards. It allowed people to figure out complex math equations. This device was made much more convenient early in China's Qing Dynasty, a period that began in 1644. One clever designer created an abacus ring that could fit on a finger. It featured beads so small they had to be moved with tiny tools such as a pin. The abacus ring had just seven wires with seven beads on each.

The invention of the **transistor** led to the creation of tiny hearing aids in the 1950s. They could be worn behind the ears. Advancements in the 1970s further shrunk the devices and brought greater clarity. Digital hearing aids invented in the 1990s were placed inside the ear and were nearly invisible to others.

Hearing aids are not the only wearable electronics to boast a long history. The first watches were created centuries earlier. The earliest of these timepieces was invented by German clockmaker Peter Henlein in the early 1500s.

The invention of digital wristwatches would have to wait for centuries. The first of these devices was invented in 1972 and sold for more than $2,000.

Though they were once cutting-edge technology, digital watches are cheap and widely available today.

They featured numbers that popped up on a screen instead of moving hands. Their popularity resulted in sales that dropped the price to $10 by the end of the decade. Soon they were so common that they were given away as prizes in cereal boxes.

There would be no free handouts of the watch introduced by Hewlett-Packard in 1977. It boasted more functions than a pocket calculator. The HP-01 featured 28 keys that could be operated with a **stylus** built into a bracelet. It allowed users to solve math

The Apple Watch is one of the most popular wearable devices.

equations. It also displayed the time and date and contained a stopwatch. This unique calculator watch, code-named Cricket, did not succeed, however. It proved too heavy for the average wrist. It was also expensive, costing up to $750. Hewlett-Packard soon removed it from the market.

The wearable electronics evolution had just begun. Watches linked to a portable television receiver hit the market in 1983. The Timex Datalink became the first watch to wirelessly download computer data in 1994. Samsung invented a watch in 1999 that people could use to see and speak with others.

The modern age had begun. Wearable electronics became known simply as wearables. They are defined as any electronic device or computer placed into clothing or accessories, such as headsets or watches. They can be worn comfortably and used all day long. These devices are often more convenient than mobile phones and laptops for performing certain computing tasks.

The potential for wearables has become almost limitless. They can influence the fields of medicine, education, transportation, gaming, music, fitness, and health. They can entertain and even save lives. They have opened up an entirely new world.

Chapter 2

The Fun Stuff

A commercial interrupts your television show. You were about to visit the kitchen to make a snack. But you notice something interesting on the screen. You sit back down. You are glued to your TV set once again.

You see actor Wesley Snipes and rapper Lil Wayne sitting on a couch and wearing headsets. Lil Wayne

Virtual reality headsets transport users into new worlds.

is concentrating. He tells his friend he cannot talk because he needs to deliver a baby elephant. He pulls his arms and hands in toward himself. In **virtual reality**, or VR, Lil Wayne has indeed brought a baby elephant to life.

VR headsets remove players from their visual environment and place them into another world. They are changing how kids and adults play games. Companies such as Sony and Samsung have created a variety of virtual reality games that require headsets. Among the most interesting is *Farpoint*, which takes users into an alien setting on the planet Jupiter. Another is *Dead Secret,* which puts players in the role of detective in a murder mystery.

Many wearables are used for video games. But others created for kids require only a wrist and imagination. They can target young and older kids, teenagers, or adults. Their purpose can be strictly fun. But perhaps the best toys and games inspire youth to explore new interests.

Among the simplest wearable toys is the Moff bracelet. It connects to a smartphone or tablet. It then creates a variety of realistic noises as kids play. The

Minecraft Wherever and Whenever

You might think this "watch" is a fitness tracker when you first see it. But it is something quite different. And it is very useful if you are a *Minecraft* player. It is the *Minecraft* Gameband. Wearing the band makes it easy to carry your *Minecraft* worlds anywhere you go. Your *Minecraft* saved data is stored on the band. You can simply take it off your wrist and plug it into any computer to start playing.

sound of tapping pencils can be heard as drumsticks. A kitchen utensil such as a whisk can sound like a tennis racket. A vivid imagination results in endless possibilities.

More complex games featuring wearables include the Playmation Marvel Avenger. The colorfully named gear strapped to the wrist is called a repulsor. The game allows players to compete inside or outside. It places them into any one of 25 missions against 20 different enemies.

Some wearables for kids have more practical uses. Among them is the VTech Kidizoom Smartwatch DX. It features a still and video camera, a voice recorder, and a voice changer. It also contains an alarm, timer, and stopwatch. The Kidizoom even boasts a calendar

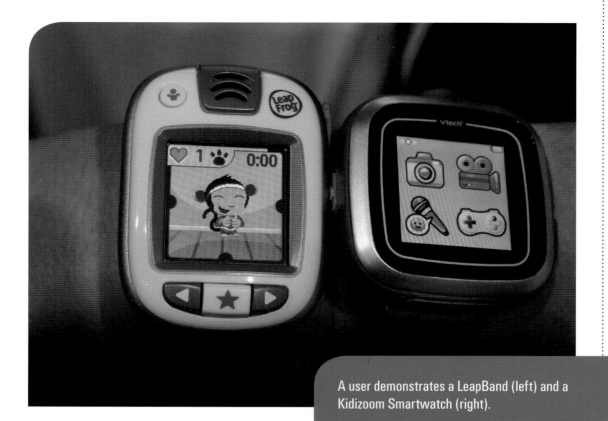

A user demonstrates a LeapBand (left) and a Kidizoom Smartwatch (right).

and calculator. Yes, it also tells time. And one need not worry about getting it wet—it is splash proof and sweatproof.

A young child without a pet at home might like to take care of one through a toy like the LeapFrog LeapBand activity tracker. This wearable toy encourages users to perform real-life movements such as "pounce like a lion." By completing these movements, players keep their virtual pets happy and healthy.

Do you want to play games with your shoes? The Skechers Game Kicks sneakers feature a built-in electronic game that wearers can enjoy anytime. Colorful buttons light up and make noise as part of a musical memory game.

The PIC is a snake-shaped camera with a bendable arm that can be attached anywhere on your body. You might attach it so it faces forward to record your hike through a beautiful outdoor area. Or you could point it behind you to give yourself a rearview camera

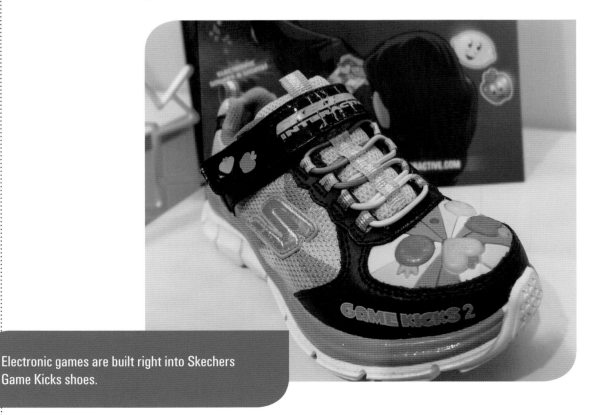

Electronic games are built right into Skechers Game Kicks shoes.

Wearable cameras allow adventurous people to record incredible footage of their activities.

as you explore. The PIC can even be utilized to record events such as concerts or football games from various angles.

The PIC is a unique toy for both kids and adults. But there is more to wearable technology than just having fun. Wearables can also help expand your mind. They have become valuable learning tools both in school and at home.

Chapter 3

Live and Learn

Y ou can visit the Great Wall of China, the Eiffel Tower in Paris, and the Nile River in Africa, all in one day. Best of all, you don't even have to leave your classroom to do it!

Welcome to Google Expeditions. This program has emerged among a new generation of headset learning tools. A folded piece of cardboard with lenses attached turns a smartphone into a virtual

Would you believe that folded cardboard and a regular smartphone are all it takes to get started with virtual reality?

Students give Google Expeditions a try at a street festival in New York City.

reality viewer. Students can really feel like they are visiting the most famous landmarks in the world.

Schools have begun to embrace wearables. The latest technology provides creative and fun ways to help kids learn a variety of subjects. Teachers like to know whether their lessons are capturing their students' attention. That is why a brain-sensing headband called Muse has gained success. Muse is equipped with seven **sensors** that track brain signals. Readings from these sensors are sent via Bluetooth to an app that translates brain activity into the sound of wind. The user hears a soft-blowing breeze when the brain is calm. An active brain results in blustery wind sounds.

Muse has been used to figure out which students lack a strong attention span. It has helped teachers learn how much interest students have in their lessons. It indicates when students are distracted or disinterested and motivates them to focus. Muse is also used outside the classroom by people who want to keep their minds as calm as possible. Unlike teachers who

Muse can help teachers figure out how to make their lessons more interesting to students.

Muse can also help people concentrate on remaining calm while meditating or relaxing in other ways.

want their students to have busy minds, these users prefer to hear calm winds coming from the Muse app.

Some students are even building their own wearable devices. British company Technology Will Save Us invented the Mover Kit because it wanted to encourage more students to learn about technology. Students use the Mover Kit to construct toys with motion sensors and lights. The toys are able to detect the students' movements and react. Building

Attracting Girls to Technology

In the past, companies that made technology and computers did not expect girls to be interested in their products. This has all changed in recent years. More women are working in technology jobs, and more girls are interested in learning about technology. As a result, many of today's wearable devices are designed to appeal to girls. For example, Jewelbots are friendship bracelets that connect to a computer or smartphone app. Wearers can write programs for their Jewelbot using computer **code**. This helps them learn the skills they will need to become computer programmers. Jewelbots also notify users when other Jewelbot wearers are nearby. This encourages them to share their ideas and discuss coding with other wearers.

these toys, and playing with them, helps students learn about electronics. It also provides an opportunity for students to create their own electronic games and inventions.

Chapter 4

For Your Health

D o you walk to school? Have you ever wondered how many steps it takes for you to reach your classroom from your front door? In the past, you might have had to count out each step you took along the way. Today, it is much simpler to use a device like Fitbit. This device is among the most popular

A wearable device can help you figure out exactly how far you walk each day.

Fitbit and other wearable health devices look a lot like watches.

wearables. It is an activity tracker that can count the number of steps you take. It can also measure heart rate, quality of sleep, and body temperature. It even uploads the information it collects to your smartphone so you can use it to develop daily fitness routines.

Making the most out of exercise helps people stay healthy. Fitbit is one of many wearables that can track the progress of activities and health goals. Another is Xmetrics, which was designed by swimmers for swimmers. The unique device attaches to swim goggles and is placed on the back of the head. It is used in a pool or any other swimming area. Xmetrics talks out loud to swimmers as they move in the water. It can count the number of strokes used to swim a certain distance. It can count laps while monitoring heart rate and quality of flip turns at the end of the pool. It can even measure how far swimmers have traveled with each stroke.

Most health-focused wearables can connect to your smartphone using special apps.

23

Gymwatch's devices help people work out hard without fear of hurting themselves.

Gymwatch makes a wearable fitness tracker called Strenx, which is worn on the arm or leg and serves as a personal trainer. It is used mostly by those who lift weights to gain strength. Strenx monitors body signals to make sure wearers are getting the most out of their workout without pushing themselves too hard. This helps them lift heavy weights with less risk of injury.

The number of health-related issues that wearables monitor continues to grow. Wearable devices can detect oxygen levels in the body. They can measure whether a person is receiving dangerous levels

The Maker of the Pacemaker

Among the most interesting figures in the history of wearable technology was Wilson Greatbatch, inventor of the pacemaker. This is an electronic device that can be implanted in a person's body to make sure the heart beats at a normal rhythm. Some people's hearts do not beat fast enough or can't keep a steady pace. Pacemakers solve this problem for them.

Greatbatch created the first pacemaker while working in his barn. It was only one of the 325 inventions he **patented** throughout his career. The pacemaker was first implanted into 10 human patients in 1960. Since then, it has helped countless people.

of the sun's rays. They can even measure the amount of pollution to which a user is exposed anytime inside or outside the home.

Many patches and sensors have been developed to monitor a variety of potential health problems. One sensor can detect heat in a wound that might signal an infection. Another can reveal stiffness in the blood vessels, which leads to heart attacks.

Other wearables help users sleep better. Through apps, smartwatches can track when users go to bed and how long they are asleep or in deep slumber. They can also monitor when users wake up and fall back asleep and detect snoring or talking as one sleeps. Some apps can also wake people up in the morning with nature sounds or soothing music.

Chapter 5

A Look into the Future

It was August 1928. The cover of a science-fiction comic book called *Amazing Stories* showed a man flying through the air with a **jetpack** strapped to his back. He was clutching a device that allowed him to travel in any direction he pleased. Kids saw the drawing as a glimpse into the future.

While jetpacks haven't exactly taken off as a popular form of travel, other wearables that seem like science fiction today could soon become everyday technology. Many of the inventors creating wearables for the future have focused on the health industry. One electronics engineer compared health wearables to the sensors used in cars—they can tell users when a part is not working correctly or is about to break down. By monitoring their health with wearable devices, people know exactly when they need to see a doctor. Researchers foresee a day when most humans are wired up with sensors that will serve as an early-warning system for dangerous medical problems.

Just as a car warns its owner when it needs maintenance, wearables could do the same for your body.

Sensors will become smaller and easier to wear. Wireless sensors mounted directly on the skin can detect body temperature, pulse, and breathing rate. The tiny sensors must be made flexible so they can stay in place while users bend and stretch.

Implants in the heart, brain, and other areas of the body could do more than detect problems. They could deliver medication whenever they sense a need. This could solve health issues from the comfort of home and even save lives.

Scientists understand that much research must be completed before sensors and implants can be reliable. But they believe every planned use is realistic. And they have already found ways to utilize them to help people stay healthy.

Advancements could also give hearing aids new uses. For example, it is believed that these devices could remind people about doctor appointments or when to take medication.

Those designing wearables of the future will also have fashion in mind. They realize that many people will not purchase wearable devices unless they are pleasing to the eye. For example, the majority of today's smartwatches are a bit bulky. But future models could look more like the fashionable watches people already enjoy wearing.

The flood of wearable electronics onto the market has just begun. Only a few companies have produced them. The result has been high prices for the consumer. But this will change in the future. A high level of competition between wearable technology companies will drive prices down.

We can be sure that the future of wearables will enhance the worlds of education, health, and gaming.

Wearables for Refrigerators?

Not all wearables of the future will be for people. Appliances such as refrigerators and ovens are already being fitted with sensors that can connect them to the Internet. Can you imagine lighting and blinds that adjust to the time of day? Refrigerators that send alerts when the milk runs out? You could even set your oven to preheat itself to 400 degrees Fahrenheit by simply talking to it. You won't have to wait long to see these situations become reality. A study predicted that one in seven homes will boast some form of smart home device by 2021.

But which devices become most popular in the future cannot be predicted. What is certain is that the seeds have been planted for a booming wearables industry that could change your life forever.

Glossary

code (KODE) instructions for a computer to follow, written in a programming language

engineer (en-juh-NEER) someone who uses knowledge of science, math, and technology to design and build solutions to practical problems

jetpack (JET-pak) a jet-powered backpack that allows users to fly through the air

odometers (oh-DAH-mih-turz) devices that measure the distance traveled

patented (PAT-uhn-tid) obtained legal proof of inventing something

sensors (SEN-surz) instruments that can detect and measure changes and transmit the information to a controlling device

stylus (STY-lus) a pen-shaped device used to input commands or drawings on a display screen

transistor (tran-ZIS-tur) a device that controls electrical flow

virtual reality (VUR-choo-uhl ree-AL-i-tee) a realistic simulation of a three-dimensional environment that is controlled by body movement

Find Out More

BOOKS

Nydal Dahl, Oyvind. *Electronics for Kids: Play with Simple Circuits and Experiment with Electricity!* San Francisco: No Starch Press, 2016.

Platt, Charles. *Make: Electronics*. San Francisco: Maker Media, 2015.

WEB SITES

CNET: Best Wearable Tech of 2017
www.cnet.com/topics/wearable-tech/best-wearable-tech
Get a look at some of the hottest wearable devices on the market right now.

Make: 10 Fabulous and Fashionable Wearable Projects from Becky Stern
www.makezine.com/2014/07/15/10-fabulous-and-fashionable -wearable-projects-from-becky-stern
Not all wearable devices are sold in stores. Find out how creative people are making their own wearables.

Index

appliances, 29

brain signals, 17–19

education, 17–19

fashion, 28
Fitbit, 21–22

games, 11, 12, 14
Google Expeditions, 16–17

health monitors, 24–25
hearing aids, 5–6, 28
Hewlett-Packard company, 7, 8

jetpacks, 26
Jewelbots, 20

Moff bracelet, 11–12
Mover Kit, 19–20

Muse headband, 17–19

pacemakers, 25
PIC camera, 14–15

Samsung, 9, 11
sensors, 17, 19, 25, 26–27, 29
sleep monitors, 25
Strenx, 24
swimming, 22–23

television, 9
transistors, 6

virtual reality, 11, 16–17
VTech Kidizoom Smartwatch DX, 12–13

watches, 6–9, 12–13, 21–22, 25, 28

About the Author

Martin Gitlin is a freelance author based in Cleveland. He has had more than 110 books published. He won more than 45 writing awards during his 11 years as a newspaper journalist, including first place for general excellence from Associated Press. That organization selected him as one of the top four feature writers in Ohio in 2001.